A Pin

by Isaac Jackson
illustrated by Marilyn Janovitz

Practice Decodable 4

McGraw Hill Education

Bothell, WA • Chicago, IL • Columbus, OH • New York, NY

MHEonline.com

Send all inquiries to:
McGraw-Hill Education
8787 Orion Place
Columbus, OH 43240

ISBN: 978-0-02-144941-5
MHID: 0-02-144941-4

Printed in the United States of America.

8 9 10 CTM 23

Lil had a pin.

Lil hid it in pants.

Dad had the pants.

The pants spin and spin!

Is a pin in the pants?

It is!